10
EVENTS
THAT CHANGED
THE WORLD

Written by Cath Senker

WAYLAND
www.waylandbooks.co.uk

Published in 2017 by Wayland
Copyright © Hodder and Stoughton, 2017

Editors: Julia Adams; Katie Woolley
Designer: Peter Clayman

Dewey number: 909-dc23
ISBN 978 0 7502 9132 3
Library eBook ISBN 978 0 7502 9128 6

Printed in China

10 9 8 7 6 5 4 3 2 1

Picture acknowledgements: Cover, p. 28 (bottom): © Sean Adair/Reuters/Corbis; p. 1, p. 3 (4th from left), p. 23: © David Turnley/ Corbis; p. 2 (far left), p. 7, p. 29 (top centre): © Historical Picture Archive/Corbis; p. 2 (2nd from left), p. 9: © The Gallery Collection/Corbis; p. 2 (3rd from left), p. 11: © The Gallery Collection/Corbis; p. 2 (4th from left), p. 5 (bottom left), p. 13, back cover (top left): © Corbis; p. 2 (5th from left), p. 15, p. 28 (centre, far right): © Corbis; p. 3 (far left), p. 5 (bottom right), p. 17, p. 29 (centre right): © Bettmann/Corbis; p. 3 (2nd from left), p. 19 (main image), back cover (bottom right): © Digital Art/Corbis; p. 3 (3rd from left), p. 4, p. 21, p. 29 (bottom): © Wolfgang Kumm/dpa/Corbis; p. 3 (5th from left): © Najlah Feanny/Corbis; p. 6: © Reuters/Corbis; p. 8: © GraphicaArtis/Corbis; p. 10: © Corbis; p. 12, p. 28 (centre): © Corbis; p. 14: © Bettmann/Corbis; p. 16: © Bettmann/Corbis; p. 18: © Bettmann/Corbis; p. 19 (inset): © Monty Rakusen/cultura/Corbis; p. 20: © Bettmann/Corbis; p. 22: © Bettmann/Corbis; p. 24: © Sergei Chirikov/epa/Corbis; p. 26 (top left): © xPACiFiCA/Corbis; p. 26 (top right): © AF-Bahrain Revolution/Demotix/Corbis; p. 26 (bottom): © Historical Picture Archive/Corbis; p. 27 (top): © Corbis; p. 27 (bottom): © Corbis; p. 28 (top): © Corbis; p. 28 (centre left): © Michael Nicholson/Corbis; p. 29 (top right): © Corbis; p. 29 (top left): © Leemage/ Corbis; all images used as graphic elements: Shutterstock.

Wayland, an imprint of Hachette Children's Group
Part of Hodder & Stoughton
Carmelite House
50 Victoria Embankment
London
EC4Y ODZ

An Hachette UK Company
www.hachette.co.uk
www.hachettechildrens.co.uk

MIX
Paper from
responsible sources
FSC® C104740
www.fsc.org

Contents

INTRODUCTION

History is full of extraordinary events that have shaped our world. Here we have chosen ten examples from the fifteenth century onwards that radically altered the lives of the people involved and those of many generations afterwards.

During the Age of Discovery from the early fifteenth century, Europeans explored the world by sea in search of new trade routes. They settled in many of the lands they found, imposing their rule on other peoples and launching an era of colonisation. European powers dominated most of the countries of Asia, Africa and the Americas until the twentieth century, when nations fought to win their independence in a series of devastating wars.

Some events marked the overthrow of a government and a dramatic shift to a new system of rule. Throughout history, revolutions have overturned the existing order and ushered in a different way of running society. The French Revolution that began in 1789 ended the feudal system under which peasants were forced to work unpaid for landowners. A few years after the Russian Revolution toppled the corrupt government of the Tsar in 1917, the Communist system developed – the government controlled the production of goods and running of services. From 1945, this system spread across eastern Europe, dividing the world between Western democracy and Soviet Communism.

Scientific developments have also changed our world. The United States of America (USA) took advantage of the invention of hugely powerful nuclear weapons to bomb Hiroshima and Nagasaki in Japan, wreaking mass destruction and ending the Second World War. Other discoveries have led to a new understanding of how the body works and advances in curing disease, such as the development of antibiotics and the decoding of DNA.

Other events triggered war: the assassination of Archduke Franz Ferdinand led to the horror of the First World War, the first truly global conflict. And Germany's invasion of Poland in 1939 was the start of the Second World War, which engulfed the world for six years.

Ten further events that have shaped our world are included on pages 26–7, and you can probably think of many more yourself!

COLUMBUS LANDS IN THE AMERICAS

On 12 October 1492, a sailor aboard the *Pinta* sighted land. Greatly excited, he alerted his captain, Christopher Columbus. Columbus was delighted to have reached India after two months' sailing from Spain. But it was not India! He had landed on what is now one of the Bahamas, the islands off the south-east coast of the USA. The local Native Americans welcomed the visitors, offering them food and water. Columbus took advantage of these peaceful people, whom he called 'Indians', and claimed possession of their island for Spain. He sailed on to take Cuba, Haiti and the Dominican Republic.

Columbus and his crew arrive in America, bearing swords.

Modern replica of Columbus's fleet set sail.

Columbus was working for the Spanish king and queen. Like other fifteenth-century European rulers, they wanted to buy spices, silk and gold from Asia. These goods were expensive because the only way to reach Asia involved a long, dangerous land journey. So they were desperate to discover a sea route to Asia. Educated people knew that the Earth was round, and Columbus thought that Asia lay about 4,800 kilometres (km) to the west of Europe. In fact, it was about 16,000 km away! Although Columbus was wrong and he had discovered America not India, the Spanish king and queen still benefited from his adventures.

> **"** They do not bear arms, and do not know them, for I showed them a sword, they took it by the edge and cut themselves out of ignorance. They have no iron. Their spears are made of cane. . . . They would make fine servants, and they are intelligent, for I saw that they repeated everything said to them. **"**
>
> CHRISTOPHER COLUMBUS, 1492

Changing the world

Columbus returned to Spain with samples of America's wealth in their payments: birds, plants, gold and native peoples. Columbus and other European explorers sailed back to the 'new world' to explore the continent and search for riches, building colonies along the way. They destroyed the local culture, forcing people to become Christians, enslaving them and spreading diseases that devastated their populations. Only small groups of Native Americans survived. This was the start of European colonisation, which continued for centuries in the Americas, Africa and Asia.

THE UNITED STATES DECLARES INDEPENDENCE

In the early 1770s, Britain ruled America and forced people to pay heavy taxes. The Americans even had to pay tax on the tea they drank every day. In 1773, a group of angry colonists had had enough. The protesters, some dressed up as Native Americans, boarded ships in Boston harbour and hurled all the chests of tea into the water, ruining an entire shipment.

This incident, known as the Boston Tea Party, followed a series of clashes between Britain and America. Britain had never ruled America closely – it was 8,000 km away and it took months to relay news back and forth. So the colonists usually sorted out their own problems. But in the 1760s, Britain had huge debts after fighting the French in Canada from 1754–63. To raise money, Britain decided that its American colonies should pay new taxes. Under the Stamp Act of 1765, Americans had to buy a stamp to attach to printed documents, such as newspapers. Furious traders refused, and Britain repealed the law. Britain then introduced the Townshend Act, placing taxes on goods such as tea and paper entering American ports. Again, many colonists would not pay, so Britain repealed this Act, too. However, the tax on tea remained.

The American Declaration of Independence is signed.

Britain continued to attempt to impose taxes, and the colonists grew angrier and angrier until in 1775 the tensions led to war. On 4 July 1776, after a year of fighting, representatives from the 13 British colonies of North America adopted the Declaration of Independence. It stated that the colonies were 'free and independent states', no longer ruled by Britain. But around one-third of the colonists remained loyal to Britain, and the war continued for five long years until Britain surrendered in 1781.

THE 13 COLONIES

The colonies that formed the USA were along the East Coast of America, from Connecticut in the north to South Carolina in the south. They were originally founded by English settlers during the seventeenth century.

Colonists hurl chests of tea overboard in protest at British taxes.

Changing the world

In 1783, a peace treaty was signed, recognising the United States of America as an independent nation. A government was established to make laws for the entire nation, and states set up their own governments. The loss of its valuable American colony was a huge defeat for the British Empire. Over the next 200 years, the United States greatly extended its own territory, and by the twentieth century became the most powerful country in the world, dominating trade across the globe and using military strength to maintain its position.

..... 1781: AMERICA WINS THE WAR OF INDEPENDENCE

THE FRENCH REVOLUTION

In 1789, the crops failed in France. The French people were starving, yet their king, King Louis XVI, basked in luxury in his palace. This was normal because eighteenth-century French society was very unequal. The nobles and clergy (churchmen) were extremely wealthy and privileged but paid no taxes. The Third Estate – ordinary people – were mostly poor, but had to pay taxes to the nobles and the church.

After this crisis, the Third Estate took a stand – they formed a National Assembly (parliament) and demanded change. The king refused, so in July 1789, the Third Estate of Paris rose up in revolution and seized the government. All around France, peasants burnt down nobles' castles and took control.

Emperor Napoleon Bonaparte took charge of France at the end of the French Revolution.

The National Assembly ended the feudal system that forced peasants to work for their landlord for nothing. It introduced the Declaration of the Rights of Man, stating that all people are born free and equal. But King Louis XVI would not obey these laws. Angered by his refusal, in 1792, protesters burst into the royal palace and captured the king and queen. To the horror of all European royalty, they executed Louis the following year.

Three new leaders ruled France through a National Convention: Georges-Jacques Danton, Jean-Paul Marat and Maximilien Robespierre. But they did not rule justly. They sent spies to seek out their enemies and killed at least 17,000 people, often chopping off their heads. Despite this 'reign of terror', which ended in 1794, these new rulers hadn't been able to control France either. In 1799, a strong leader called Napoleon toppled the government, and in 1804 declared himself Napoleon I, Emperor of France. The era of upheaval was over.

JUNE 1789: NATIONAL ASSEMBLY IS FORMED ..... 14 JULY: PARIS PROTESTERS

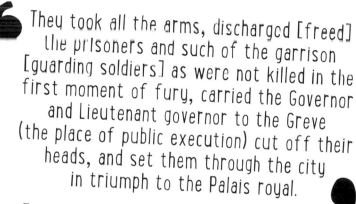

> 66 They took all the arms, discharged [freed] the prisoners and such of the garrison [guarding soldiers] as were not killed in the first moment of fury, carried the Governor and Lieutenant governor to the Greve (the place of public execution) cut off their heads, and set them through the city in triumph to the Palais royal. 99
>
> **Thomas Jefferson, America's minister to France, witnessed the attack on the Bastille prison to seize arms on 14 July 1789**

Changing the world

Although France was ruled by one strong leader once more, it did not return to the same kind of unequal society as before. Revolutionary ideas spread to other lands. In the early nineteenth century, Latin American countries fought and won their independence from Spain and Portugal. For example, in Venezuela, revolutionary leader Simón Bolívar greatly admired the French Revolution. In Europe, Karl Marx and Friedrich Engels developed the ideas of Communism, drawing on the experience of the French Revolution. It inspired further uprisings, including revolutions across Europe in 1848 and the Russian Revolution of 1917.

ARCHDUKE FRANZ FERDINAND OF AUSTRIA IS ASSASSINATED

It was a beautiful summer's day on 28 June 1914, as the motorcade with Archduke Franz Ferdinand, nephew of the Emperor of Austria-Hungary, passed through the streets of Sarajevo, Bosnia. The archduke and his wife, Sophie, waved at the crowds from their open-topped limousine. At one point, the driver slowed. Assassin Gavrilo Princip rushed forward and fired two shots, fatally wounding Franz Ferdinand and Sophie.

Archduke Ferdinand and his wife touring Sarajevo, just before their assassination.

The killer was a Serb nationalist, who believed that Serbs in Bosnia should break free of Austro-Hungarian rule and govern Bosnia themselves. The furious Austro-Hungarian emperor blamed Serbia for the crime and, exactly one month later, declared war on Serbia. Both sides sought allies. Serbia joined forces with Russia, France and Britain, while Austria-Hungary was allied with Germany and Italy. Within weeks, Europe was engulfed in war.

Why did so many other countries become involved? During the nineteenth century, European countries had developed a strong sense of nationalism – they were proud of their country but often hostile towards others. Germany wanted to protect itself from any revenge attack by France, which it had defeated in the 1870–71 war. It made pacts with Austria-Hungary and Italy. France, Britain and Russia made an alliance to counter the threat from Germany's group. Now, a threat to one country meant its allies were likely to become involved, too.

Other tensions arose over empires. Britain and France ruled parts of Asia and Africa. From the late nineteenth century, Germany started to carve out its own empire in Africa, angering Britain and France. Within Europe, Austria-Hungary and Russia competed fiercely for influence in the Balkans.

FIRST WORLD WAR DEATHS

Around 9.5 million soldiers died from wounds or disease.

Around 13 million civilians died from disease, starvation or military actions.

Canadian troops, allied to Britain, charge out of their trench during the First World War, 1916.

Changing the world

The First World War lasted for four years, involved most European countries and resulted in the fall of the Austro-Hungarian, Russian, German and Ottoman empires. The mechanisation of warfare – the development of machinery to kill people on a massive scale – transformed the way wars were fought. Armies used tanks, machine guns, bomber planes, torpedoes (underwater missiles) and poison gas. The number of casualties dwarfed those of all previous wars and, unlike in earlier wars, millions of civilians were also displaced and killed.

GERMANY INVADES POLAND

It was just before dawn on 1 September 1939. With no warning or declaration of war, 1.5 million German soldiers in tanks, on horseback and on foot invaded Poland. German planes rained incendiary bombs on Polish cities. As the air-raid sirens sounded in the capital, Warsaw, citizens gazed in astonishment at the skies. They were witnessing the first demonstration of German blitzkrieg – lightning war.

The Nazi German leader Adolf Hitler was taking a gamble. He believed his forces would quickly defeat the Polish army and did not think Britain and France would challenge him. In 1938, Germany had united with Austria and seized the Sudetenland from Czechoslovakia. Most people in France and Britain accepted Germany's actions, believing German power was a useful counterforce to the Communist Soviet Union. In the same year, Hitler made the Munich Agreement with British Prime Minister Neville Chamberlain, stating that he would seize no further land.

Italian leader Benito Mussolini, Hitler, an interpreter and Chamberlain (from left) at the Munich conference, 1938.

However, in March 1939 Hitler's troops occupied the whole of Czechoslovakia and prepared to invade Poland. Realising that an attack on Poland could trigger war with its neighbour, the Soviet Union, Hitler made a surprise pact with the Soviet Union in August. They promised not to go to war against each other and secretly agreed to occupy Poland and divide it between them.

1 SEPTEMBER 1939, 04:45: GERMANY INVADES POLAND ..... 09:00: GERMANY BOMBS

> " . . . all of a sudden some [Polish] soldiers appeared asking for civilian clothes to change into with the hopes that they wouldn't be captured as prisoners. They remarked, 'We are lost. Poland doesn't have the necessary weapons to protect itself. The Nazis are very well armed, motorised, with tanks and everything else.'"
>
> Eyewitness in Polish border town Działoszyn, 1 September 1939

German soldiers march confidently through Poland during the 1939 invasion.

Changing the world

Hitler had misjudged his enemies, when German troops invaded Poland. Britain and France declared war on Germany. Within weeks, Germany had taken control of most of Poland. The following year, Germany took control of Denmark, Norway, Belgium, the Netherlands, Luxembourg and France. Over the following years, war engulfed Europe, the Soviet Union, Asia and the Pacific, killing 40 million people. It was to be the bloodiest war in history.

ATOMIC-BOMB ATTACKS ON HIROSHIMA AND NAGASAKI

On 6 August 1945, a US bomber dropped the first atomic bomb ever used in warfare on Hiroshima in Japan. Exploding 580 metres above the ground, it created a giant mushroom cloud of smoke and fire. Around 70,000 people died instantly – many bodies simply melted in the intense heat. The explosion flattened more than 10 square km (6 miles) of Hiroshima and caused fires that burned for three days, trapping and killing thousands of people. Three days later, the USA dropped an even larger bomb on Nagasaki, instantly killing about 40,000 people and destroying one-third of the city.

The Second World War in Europe had ended back in May 1945 but the conflict in East Asia between the Allies and Japan continued. The Allies believed that an attack on Japan using regular weapons would be lengthy and cause huge casualties, while using a nuclear weapon would be so devastating that it would finish the war quickly. The US Army selected Hiroshima and Nagasaki because the first was an important military base and the second a large port. The attacks did indeed ensure Japan's defeat. On 14 August, Japan surrendered on the Allies' terms. The war was over.

A scene of total devastation after the bombing of Hiroshima.

COUNTRIES KNOWN TO HAVE NUCLEAR WEAPONS AND THE NUMBER OF NUCLEAR WARHEADS, 2014

USA: 4,804
Russia: about 1,500
France: fewer than 300
China: about 250
United Kingdom: up to 225
Israel: 75-200
Pakistan: 100-120
India: 90-110

6 AUGUST 1945: USA DROPS AN ATOMIC BOMB ON HIROSHIMA .... 9 AUGUST:

A giant mushroom cloud rises above Nagasaki as the atomic bomb strikes the city.

Changing the world

After the war, tens of thousands of Japanese people died agonising deaths from radiation sickness. Despite the evidence of mass devastation caused by nuclear weapons, the USA and the Soviet Union (which were now competing superpowers) built up their nuclear forces, arguing that they were needed for defence. Not all agreed with this approach; an international peace movement grew in the 1950s, calling for the banning of nuclear weapons. But powerful countries continued to develop them. No nuclear bomb has ever been used since Hiroshima and Nagasaki, although the USA and the Soviet Union came dangerously close to doing so during the Cuban missile crisis of 1962. As of 2014, eight countries were known to have nuclear weapons, so the world still lives with the threat of nuclear conflict.

DISCOVERING THE 'SECRET OF LIFE'

28 February 1953 was one of the best days of scientist James Watson's life. He recalled, 'At lunch Francis winged in to the Eagle [a Cambridge pub] to tell everyone within hearing distance that we had found the secret of life.' Watson and fellow Cambridge University scientist Francis Crick had just discovered the structure of DNA, solving one of the main mysteries of genetics. DNA contains the genes that are passed on from parent to child, determining many features, such as eye colour, and helping to make us how we are. Crick and Watson showed that DNA is a double-helix shape and explained how it copies itself.

Crick and Watson had spent months testing out models for DNA but had not carried out any experiments to provide evidence for them. Other scientists were working on the problem, too. At King's College, London, Rosalind Franklin was undertaking lengthy and complicated work taking X-ray photos of DNA to try to discover its structure through careful analysis.

Maurice Wilkins studies a DNA model after receiving the Nobel Prize.

In December 1952, a colleague, Maurice Wilkins, secretly showed Watson Franklin's data and an X-ray photo indicating what DNA would look like if the model was correct. Wilkins knew this would have angered Franklin. The data provided Crick and Watson with vital evidence. Yet when they announced their findings, they failed to thank Franklin. Crick, Watson and Wilkins received the Nobel Prize for Science in 1962, gaining their place in scientific history. Rosalind Franklin had died in 1958, and her contribution was not acknowledged until much later.

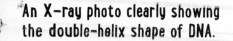

An X-ray photo clearly showing the double-helix shape of DNA.

A scientist undertakes DNA research in the lab.

Changing the world

The knowledge of DNA's structure opened up a range of scientific fields, from medical treatment to food production and solving crime. In the 1970s, scientists worked out how to genetically modify micro-organisms to make human hormones and in 1978, they made insulin for people with diabetes. By 2003, scientists working on the Human Genome Project had worked out the whole sequence of human DNA. Doctors can now test people's DNA to see if they are likely to develop certain diseases, such as cancer, and researchers are developing gene replacement therapy to replace faulty genes. In agriculture, scientists have created genetically engineered foods, for example, tomatoes that do not rot quickly. Police forces can take DNA samples from suspected criminals to see if it matches DNA at the scene of a crime. The 1953 discoveries made all these breakthroughs possible.

TEARING DOWN THE BERLIN WALL

On 9 November 1989, thousands of East Germans smashed down the Berlin Wall and poured through to West Berlin to start a new life in democratic Western Europe.

Since 1949, Germany had been divided and the capital city of Berlin torn in two. West Berlin was part of West Germany, a Western democracy. East Berlin was in Communist-ruled East Germany and allied to the Soviet Union. West Germany was far wealthier than the East, with better-paid jobs and a higher standard of living. From 1939 to 1961, more than 2 million East Germans fled to the West.

Hole in the wall: policemen examine a bomb blast probably caused by East Berlin protest groups, May 1962.

One night, in August 1961, the East German government rapidly erected a wall between East and West Berlin to prevent further escapes. Once completed, the wall formed a vast concrete barrier, 3.6 metres (12 feet) high, topped with barbed wire. Armed guards surveyed the border from watchtowers and mines were buried in the ground, ready to explode and kill escapees. From 1961 to 1989, 5,000 people were caught trying to escape, and 191 lost their lives in their attempts. Nevertheless, during that time, 5,000 East Germans succeeded in crossing safely to the West.

By 1989, a democracy movement was flowing through Eastern Europe, and in October, the Communist East German government was swept from power. On 9 November, the borders between East and West Berlin were opened.

> " People helped each other; some lifted, others pulled. All along the building, people poured up the wall. At the Berlin Wall itself, which is 3 metres high, people had climbed up and were sitting astride [it]. The final slab was moved away. A stream of East Germans began to pour through. People applauded and slapped their backs. "

Andreas Ramos had driven from Denmark to witness the event

Celebrating the opening of the Berlin Wall at New Year, 1990.

Changing the world

The fall of the Berlin Wall was a significant event in the surge of democratic movements that toppled the Communist Eastern European governments of Poland, Hungary, Czechoslovakia and the Soviet Union in 1989–91. The Soviet Union split up into individual countries, which switched to Western-style market economies. While people had more freedom, a huge division developed between rich and poor in the former Communist countries.

NELSON MANDELA IS FREED

On 11 February 1990, crowds of black and white South Africans gathered outside the gates of Victor Verster Prison near Cape Town. They eagerly awaited the release of the world's most famous prisoner, 71-year-old political leader Nelson Mandela. Finally, a little after 4 pm, Mandela walked free after 27 years in jail. He and his wife, Winnie, strode through the cheering crowds, raising their fists in the air in the black freedom salute.

Nelson Mandela was a leader of the African National Congress (ANC), which opposed the apartheid system and fought for democracy. In South Africa, white people made up just one-fifth of the population but had total power and the best jobs, education, health care and public facilities available. The black majority could not vote and lived in the poorest areas in bad conditions. The government tried to crush all opposition, declaring the ANC illegal in 1960 and imprisoning many activists.

SOUTH AFRICA STATS

Percentage of black population enrolled in secondary education

1994 51%   2014 80%

Percentage of black population with access to running water

1994/5 60%   2011/12 95%

Percentage of black population with access to electricity

1994/5 50%   2012/13 86%

Mandela walks proudly out of prison to a welcoming crowd.

Children play in a desperately poor black area of Johannesburg, 1955.

During the 1970s and 1980s, the anti-apartheid campaign in South Africa and around the world grew and grew, and the country erupted in protest, strikes and violence. Eventually, the white government realised it had no choice but to lift the ban on the ANC and negotiate a peaceful settlement with its former enemies.

Changing the world

After Mandela's release, all the apartheid laws were abolished. In 1994, millions of South Africans voted in the first democratic elections; the ANC was victorious and Nelson Mandela became the country's first black president. Nations around the world that had refused to trade or play sports with South Africa in protest against apartheid now restored relations with the country. South Africa rejoined the international organisation, the United Nations (UN), in 1994. Instead of fighting with its African neighbours, South Africa now played a positive role, pushing for negotiations to end conflicts across the continent. Twenty years on, despite problems of high unemployment, crime and HIV infection, South Africa is still a democracy, and millions more people have access to education, housing, water and electricity than under apartheid.

9/11: TWIN TOWERS TERROR ATTACKS

On 11 September 2001, hijackers seized control of two commercial aircraft. Minutes later, the horrified passengers realised they were to be used as 'flying bombs', to be aimed and flown directly into the twin towers of the World Trade Center in New York. The towers burst into flames on impact, and floor by floor, they crumpled to the ground. Another hijacked plane slammed into the Pentagon, the US military headquarters in Washington, D.C.. Over 3,000 people lost their lives on that fateful day. It was the deadliest terrorist attack ever on US soil.

DEATHS IN THE ATTACKS

New York: 2,750

Pentagon: 184

Pennsylvania: 40

Emergency workers: over 400

The USA attacks Afghanistan, October 2001.

The 19 hijackers were linked to the radical Islamic group, Al-Qaeda. Fifteen of the bombers were from Saudi Arabia, the same country as Osama Bin Laden, who was widely seen as their leader. Al-Qaeda believed that the USA had too much influence over the Saudi government and was angry that US troops were stationed in Muslim Saudi Arabia. It wanted to end Western involvement in the Islamic world. Al-Qaeda turned to violent tactics to focus the world's attention on the issues and try to force change.

> 66 You heard a big boom, it was quiet for about ten seconds. Then you could hear another one. Now I realise it was the floors starting to stack on top of each other as they were falling. It was spaced apart in the beginning, but then it got to just a tremendous roar and a rumble that I will never forget. 99
>
> Neil Sweeting, New York paramedic

The Twin Towers collapse in smoke and flames.

Changing the world

The large-scale death and destruction wreaked by 9/11 had the opposite effect to the one Al-Qaeda had wanted. The US government became determined to increase its influence in Muslim countries and combat terrorism worldwide. It went to great lengths to root out suspected Al-Qaeda radicals and imprison them. Within weeks, the USA and Britain, with support from other Western nations, launched a military attack on Afghanistan, where they believed Al-Qaeda was based. The war on terror became the main aim of US foreign policy for years to come, leading to conflicts in countries including Iraq, Pakistan and Yemen, and many thousands more deaths.

10 OTHER EVENTS THAT CHANGED THE WORLD

1. Christianity is born

In around 30 CE, the preacher Jesus was executed. His followers believed that he rose from the dead and was the Son of God, and they converted others to their faith in him. This was the beginning of Christianity, which became a major world religion.

2. The last Roman emperor falls

The Roman emperor Romulus Augustulus fell from power in 476 CE. ending the Western Roman Empire. The Roman Empire had lasted for nearly 500 years. The Eastern Roman. or Byzantine Empire. continued for another 1.000 years until 1453. Roman culture has influenced Western culture right down to the present day.

3. The Hijrah

In seventh-century Arabia. most people believed in many gods, but the prophet Muhammad from Mecca preached that there was only one God. Many people in Mecca were hostile to Muhammad, so in 622, he and his followers left for Medina to establish the Islamic faith, which spread quickly to become one of the world's main religions. Muhammad's journey became known as the Hijrah.

4. The First Crusade

The First Crusade in 1095 was the first of a series of military campaigns during which Christians travelled from Europe to the Middle East to fight the Muslim rulers for control of places such as Jerusalem. which were holy to Christians, Jews and Muslims. By 1291, the Muslims had won them back again. Tensions in the region between the three faiths still exist today.

5. The Black Death

Reaching Europe from Asia in 1348, this deadly plague killed nearly everyone affected within days. It spread across the continent and killed up to half of the population by 1350. The high death toll had a huge impact on European society.

6. Edward Jenner discovers vaccination

In 1796, English surgeon Jenner worked out that if you injected people with a weak form of a disease, they would gain immunity (protection) from a more serious form. He developed a vaccine for the deadly disease smallpox by injecting people with the milder cowpox. Vaccination revolutionised medicine, allowing people to be protected against many life-threatening diseases, and saving millions of lives.

7. Wright Brothers' first flight

In 1903, brothers Wilbur and Orville Wright from the USA built and flew the first aeroplane with a motor. Their design formed the basis for the development of modern aircraft, which allowed people to travel further and faster than ever before.

8. The Russian Revolution

The 1917 Russian Revolution took place in two stages and ended the harsh rule of the Tsars, or emperors. In 1922, the Soviet Union was established as the world's first Communist state. The government took control of all the land, resources and production of goods. After the Second World War, Communism was imposed on Eastern Europe, leading to the Cold War between the Communist bloc and Western democracies.

9. India gains independence

In the early twentieth century, Mahatma Gandhi led a movement to demand independence from British rule. Britain finally granted it in 1947. Most other Asian and African countries achieved independence from European control over the following thirty years.

10. The Moon landing

On 21 July 1969, US astronaut Neil Armstrong was the first person to walk on the Moon. The Moon landing marked the peak of the space race between the USA and the Soviet Union, which had competed to put a man on the Moon. Since then, many manned and unmanned spacecraft have been launched into space to advance our knowledge of the universe.

TIMELINE

476
The fall of the last Roman Emperor, Romulus Augustulus, leads to the decline of the Roman Empire.

1215
In England, the Magna Carta is signed, an agreement that states that the king of England has to follow the law and gives rights to the English people.

1917
The Russian Revolution takes place in Russia, ending the rule of the Tsars and leading to a Communist government.

1914
The First World War breaks out after the assassination of Archduke Franz Ferdinand.

1939
The Second World War begins when Germany invades Poland, and Britain and France declare war on Germany.

2001
Members of a terrorist group called Al-Qaeda hijack four aeroplanes in the USA and fly two of them into the World Trade Center in New York and one at the Pentagon; a fourth one crashes in a field. About 3,000 are killed.

1492
The explorer Christopher Columbus arrives in the Americas and claims several Caribbean islands for Spain.

1776
The United States declares independence from Britain and sets up its own government.

1865
The American Civil War between the Northern and Southern states ends with the victory of the North.

1789
The French Revolution breaks out, overturning the king and queen and a republic to govern the country is set up.

1945
The USA drops atomic bombs on Hiroshima and Nagasaki, killing tens of thousands of people instantly and leading to the end of the Second World War.

1949
Communist leader Mao Zedong takes control of China and forms the People's Republic of China.

1989
The East German government is forced out of power, the borders are opened with West Germany, and the Berlin Wall between East and West Berlin is torn down.

1969
The USA lands a spacecraft on the moon: Neil Armstrong and Buzz Aldrin are the first men to walk on the moon.

GLOSSARY

abolish Formally put an end to something.

alliance An agreement between countries, for example, to work together in order to achieve something that they all want.

Allies The countries, including France and Britain, that were allies during the first and second world wars.

ally A country that has agreed to help and support another country, especially if it goes to war.

apartheid The former political system in South Africa in which only white people had full political rights and non-white people were forced to live in separate areas and use their own schools, hospitals etc.

assassination To murder an important person, especially for political reasons.

colonisation When a country takes control of another area or country, especially using force, and sends people from its country to live there – those people are called colonists.

colony A country or an area that is governed by people from another, more powerful, country.

Communism A political system in which the government controls the production of goods and the running of services.

counterforce A force that acts in opposition to another force.

democracy A political system in which all adults can vote in elections for the rulers of the country.

diabetes A medical condition in which a person's blood sugar levels can become too high.

DNA The chemical in the cells of animals and plants that carries genetic information.

emperor The ruler of an empire or a group of countries or states.

enslave To make someone into a slave, who works for their master without being paid.

execute To kill somebody, especially as a punishment for breaking the law.

feudal To do with the system where landowners owned land and peasants were allowed to work on it in return for service to their landlord.

genetics The scientific study of the ways in which different features, such as eye colour, are passed from parents to their children.

hijacker Someone who illegally seizes control of an aircraft.

HIV A virus that damages the immune system (the body's defences against disease) so that the sufferer catches diseases easily. If no treatment is given, an HIV infection causes AIDS.

hormone A chemical substance produced in the body or in a plant that encourages growth or influences how the body works.

incendiary bomb A bomb designed to cause a fire.

insulin A chemical substance produced in the body that controls the amount of sugar in the blood.

invasion When an army from one country enters another country by force to take control of it.

micro-organism A very small living thing that you can only see under a microscope.

motorcade A procession of motor vehicles.

nationalism A feeling of pride in your country, which can also mean you believe that your country is better than any other. People who believe in nationalism are called nationalists.

noble Of a high rank in society and often rich.

nuclear weapon A weapon using nuclear energy. Matter is turned into energy by splitting the nuclei, the central part of atoms. Nuclear energy is extremely powerful.

occupy To enter an area or country and take control of it, especially by force.

pact An agreement between people or countries, especially one in which they agree to help each other.

peace treaty An agreement between two hostile countries that formally ends a state of war.

peasant A farmer who owns or rents a small piece of land.

Pentagon The building near Washington, D.C. that is the headquarters of the US Department of Defence and the military leaders.

radiation Powerful and very dangerous rays that are sent out from radioactive substances, for example, from a nuclear bomb.

radical Believing in a complete political or social change of some kind, for example, radical Muslims believe in an extreme form of Islamic rule.

repeal To stop a law.

revolution An attempt, by a large number of people, to change the government of a country, especially by violent action.

superpower A country that has great military or economic power and great influence; from 1945 to 1991, the USA and the Soviet Union were the two world superpowers.

surrender In war, to admit that you have been beaten and agree to stop fighting.

terrorist A person who uses violent actions to achieve political aims.

trade route A pathway used to transport goods around the world.

FURTHER INFORMATION

Book

The Top Ten: Events That Changed the World, Anita Ganeri (Franklin Watts, 2011)

Websites

Christopher Columbus:
www.bbc.co.uk/schools/primaryhistory/famouspeople/christopher_columbus

The Declaration of Independence:
www.congressforkids.net/Independence_declaration_1.htm

The French Revolution:
www.bbc.co.uk/bitesize/ks3/history/uk_through_time/popular_protest_through_time/revision/6/

Assassination of Franz Ferdinand:
www.historyonthenet.com/ww1/assassination.htm

Germany invades Poland:
www.bbc.co.uk/history/worldwars/wwtwo/invasion_poland_01.shtml

The bombing of Hiroshima and Nagasaki:
http://history1900s.about.com/od/worldwarii/a/hiroshima.htm

Discovering the structure of DNA:
www.ducksters.com/science/biology/dna.php

Nelson Mandela:
www.bbc.co.uk/schools/primaryhistory/famouspeople/nelson_mandela/

The Twin Towers attacks:
www.bbc.co.uk/newsround/14854813

INDEX